'Night, America

To Kathy and Ross

Library of Congress Cataloging-in-Publication Data

Montgomery, Michael, 1952–
'Night, America / written and illustrated by Michael Montgomery.
24 p.   cm.   "A Calico book."
Summary: A poetic "good night" to the President, the Chicago Cubs,
and NASA astronauts.
ISBN 0-8092-4397-0
1. Night—Juvenile poetry.   2. Children's poetry, American.
[1. Bedtime—Poetry.   2. American poetry.]   I. Title.
II. Title: Goodnight, America.   III. Title: Good night, America.
PS3563.05454N54   1989
811'.54—dc19   88-8533   CIP   AC

Published by Contemporary Books, Inc.
180 North Michigan Avenue, Chicago, Illinois 60601
Manufactured in the United States of America
Library of Congress Catalog Card Number: 88-8533
International Standard Book Number: 0-8092-4397-0

Published simultaneously in Canada by Beaverbooks, Ltd.
195 Allstate Parkway, Valleywood Business Park
Markham, Ontario L3R 4T8 Canada

E
MOH

'Night, America

Written and Illustrated by

MICHAEL MONTGOMERY

A CALICO BOOK

Published by Contemporary Books, Inc.

CHICAGO · NEW YORK

'Night, Prairies

'Night, Cowboys

'Night, Astronauts

'Night, Mr. President

'Night, Chicago Cubs

'Night, Golden Gate Bridge

'Night, Redwoods

'Night, My Town

'Night, Everyone